J R LOPEZ

JUMP START

REAL LIFE ADVICE FOR THE NERVOUS LEARNER DRIVER

Contents

"It's not the mountain we conquer, but ourselves."

-Edmund Hillary

Introduction

Based on my own experience as a reluctant learner driver, this book is intended to guide and empower you. I know how it feels to dread every lesson. I've cried in front of my instructor. I'm all too familiar with feeling sick to my stomach on the day of my driving test. Even the mere thought of driving would leave me with crippling anxiety and panic attacks. This book is about the all things I wish I'd known, and how I overcame my nerves and anxiety to finally take control of my driving lessons.

There are two things I think are really important to remember:

1. You don't know how to drive

Why would you need lessons if you already know how to drive? My first instructor assumed I knew what I was doing for the majority of the time, and due to my lack of confidence, I rarely questioned him. There wasn't much teaching going on. It seemed as though I was expected to just get the hang of it if we drove around for long enough. I didn't.

2. You are the customer

If you are paying for professional driving lessons, you are a customer. You should have a say on how your lessons are planned and taught, and have the right to expect a certain level of service.

"Everybody is a genius. But if you judge a fish by its ability to climb a tree, it will live its whole life believing that it is stupid."

– Albert Einstein

Chapter 1. My driving story

When I was about twelve years old, my brother and I sat in the back of our parent's car, as we waited at a red light. Unaware of the other vehicle hurtling towards us, the first we knew of it was when it smashed in to the back of us. Luckily, we were all wearing seatbelts, and the worse we suffered was a sense of shock, whiplash and bruising. The driver and his passenger got out and ran, and it later transpired that the car they were driving was stolen.

I didn't think much of it at the time, but when I look back over the years, it's clear to me that this was one of several events that began to shape how I felt about being in control of a car. That incident alone may have passed by with little consequence had it been a one off, but several further events compounded and confirmed my fear of driving.

As a teenager, my boyfriend was a reckless driver. His default mode was aggressive, and road rage was a regular feature of most journeys. He was also careless, and on one occasion, he pulled out of a side street without checking to see if the road was clear. It wasn't, and a car crashed in to the side of us, spinning the car a couple of times, my head ricocheting off the window. Again, whiplash and concussion.

A few months later, he was driving me home from a friend's house. A white mini-van cut in front of us, and unable to let it go he sped after him. When he caught up, he turned the car around so that both driver's windows were adjacent and wound his window down. He launched into an expletive driven rant at the van driver, who wound his own window down, leant forward and spat at us through the open window. Then both men were out on the street, throwing punches. My pleas to stop were ignored and in a fit of rage my boyfriend smashed a window of the van. That brought things to a head, and shocked at his own appalling behaviour, he agreed to pay for the damage. But it seems we were followed home, as the next day he woke to find his car covered in white emulsion.

We soon went our separate ways, but I felt pretty shaken by that incident and his many other bouts of road rage left me feeling on edge. Much of the fear I had about driving, involved thoughts about what would happen if I did something wrong. In my mind, I could only picture my car journey ending in fireball of a car crash, or at best a terrifying confrontation with another driver's road rage. Neither seemed particularly appealing, so I decided the best thing would be to just avoid driving altogether. Much safer.

I didn't want to learn to drive. But society places such importance and reverence on being able to do it, and so I did reluctantly agree to lessons, and began a miserable few years of anxiety and failure behind the wheel. After the third failed attempt I eventually gave it up as a lost cause, and resigned myself to a life of public transport and using my own two feet to get where I needed to be. And actually that worked out fine for quite a while. As a student a car would have been an expense I couldn't afford, and most of my fellow students didn't drive, so I didn't feel like the odd one out. When I graduated, I did a few temp jobs and a short while later found myself a job in New York. I lived there for the next two years, where owning a car is really completely unnecessary. So again, not a problem, and on returning to the UK, I moved to a fairly big city with a mostly reliable system of buses and trains.

As time went on and I got a bit older, I began to feel a sense of judgement when it cropped up in conversation that I couldn't drive. Often people had no problem telling me it was weird, or that I really should have learnt by now. It really started to grind my gears when people asked why I didn't drive. At work it began to feel like an issue, and I felt like a child having to rely on colleagues to take to me to meetings or work events. If I thought about driving, I would feel anxious. Whenever I pictured myself driving, it always ended with me losing control, crashing and killing myself. If friends or colleagues broached the idea of taking lessons, I changed the subject and shut down the conversation.

And then, about fifteen years after taking those first lessons, my Dad gently suggested he might buy me some driving lessons for my birthday. By this time, my circumstances had changed somewhat, which meant that getting around had become a little more difficult. I decided to accept my Dad's offer. If I only took those first lessons and did nothing more, then so be it. I decided to tell no-one apart from my parents and a few close friends, and that this time around, I'd be the one in control ☺

"Whether you think you can, or you think you can't, you're right."

– Henry Ford

Chapter 2. Coping with nerves and anxiety

I'd reached a point where the mere thought of driving left me in a state of anxiety. Every time I pictured myself in charge of a car, I'd see myself panicking and crashing. I wouldn't enter in to conversations about learning. It left me feeling sick with worry and cringing with embarrassment. Clearly this was more than just nerves.

Driving Phobia

When does a natural fear of something cross over into being a phobia?

The NHS defines a phobia as:

"an overwhelming and debilitating fear of an object, place, situation, feeling or animal. Phobias are more pronounced than fears. They develop when a person has an exaggerated or unrealistic sense of danger about a situation or object."

In my case, I can pick out the incidents that most likely contributed to my irrational fear and unwillingness to learn. The wrong instructor, a lack of confidence, a couple of accidents and a traumatic road rage incident meant that driving, or even thinking about driving, became extremely anxiety inducing. Being able to attribute these feelings and fears to actual past events, helped to give me some perspective.

However, the reason for a phobia may not always be so obvious. Anxiety Care UK talks about a fear or phobia of driving as being part of a general anxiety disorder, and that if the cause of this fear is not immediately obvious, it might be more beneficial to deal with your symptoms, rather than trying to establish the root course. With that in mind, I tried to develop some key coping mechanisms and techniques to overcome my negative thoughts.

Empower yourself

The thing that really changed everything for me was the realisation that I could be in control of this situation. If at any point I wanted to stop learning I could. I could take a break. I could ask for more lessons. I could choose to never drive for my whole life if I wanted to, or I could take the test and see what happened. I shifted my perspective from seeing myself as a passive student and the instructor as a judgemental teacher, to two professional people on an equal footing. I had found someone with the expertise I needed to help me learn this new skill, and decided I would now be a much more active learner, asking questions and contributing to the process. This wasn't an easy transition, and I had to tell myself this over and over, until at some point the nerves and dread I felt before each lesson started to ease a little.

Nerves aren't all bad

Feeling nervous is normal. But it is possible to control and channel your nerves to your advantage.

We've always been told that stress is bad for us, but while I was learning to drive, I came across the idea that we can use the way our bodies respond to stress, to not only cope with the situation we find ourselves in, but in some cases actually improve our performance. I'd seen a TV show where a man with severe anxiety and fear of heights was guided to walk over a bridge suspended high in the air. As his panic grew, the person supporting him encouraged him to take notice of how he was feeling, and recognise that his body was producing an extra surge in energy to conquer the task ahead of him. Increased heart rate, rapid breathing, dilated pupils; these are all symptoms of a panic attack, but they are also all symptoms of the adrenaline rush we get when we're about to do something exciting or scary for the first time. I'd never thought about the way stress makes me feel before, and how to take notice of those feelings and reframe them from a negative response to a positive one. As soon as I felt the panic rise, I would tell myself, out loud if necessary, that my racing heart beat was adrenaline, and my body's way of preparing me for the challenge ahead. By changing how I viewed the symptoms of stress, I was able to take control of it and use it to my advantage.

Fake it 'til you make it

When you're feeling a lack of confidence or think you can't do something, *pretend* that you can. Channel your inner drama skills and act as if you've got the confidence you need. If you do that for long enough the nerves fade in to the background while you're concentrating on pretending to be confident, and after a while that confidence becomes genuine.

And don't underestimate the benefits of positive affirmations. You might feel a bit ridiculous at first, but tell yourself out loud what a brilliant, confident person you are, and that you're capable of achieving anything you put your mind to. What have you got to lose?

Take it one lesson at a time

Unfortunately, I have a tendency to catastrophize. I think about a stressful situation and my mind takes me to the worst possible ending of that scenario. When considering learning to drive I found myself jumping ahead through time to the day of the test, or being alone having passed and feeling how stressful that would be. All before I'd even signed up for the first lesson.

Tell yourself that all you're doing for now is taking the first lesson. No-one is going to force you to take the next one, or even take the test. Just go through one lesson at a time, and only focus on that one lesson. As humans we seem to be good at giving other people advice. So if you find your mind racing ahead to future negative scenarios, you mind find it helpful to talk to yourself out loud, as if you were advising a friend. Or if you feel self-conscious doing that, write it down. Tell yourself that negative thoughts are unhelpful, and then refocus your mind to the one lesson you have planned that week.

Talk to someone

For a long time, I held the misconception that everyone else loved driving, and that they were all really good at it. But once you open up about it, you'll see that many other people feel the same way as you do. However, if your fear or phobia is deep rooted, you may need to talk to someone who is qualified to give you the help you need, especially if your fear of driving is part of a wider anxiety disorder. This book is intended to help and guide you, based on my own experiences and those of people close to me, but it's not a replacement for the advice that a trained professional can give you. You can start by talking with your GP, and I've also listed some helpful resources at the end of this book.

"When you realize how much you're worth, you'll stop giving people discounts."

– Karen Salmansohn

Chapter 3. Choosing your instructor

Finding the right driving instructor for you is essential. You need to feel confident in their teaching and comfortable in their company. You're going to be spending a lot of time together, with the aim being to come away from each lesson feeling as though you have learnt something, rather than already dreading the next one. Even if you already have an instructor, you might find the following information helpful. Just because you already have one, they may not necessarily be the right one for you.

Finding an instructor.

I chose my first instructor because he had taught my friend, and she had passed first time. What I didn't consider was that my friend and I are very different people in terms of how we learn, and the level of confidence we have behind the wheel. She breezed through her lessons and her test, while every lesson for me was one painful disaster after another, not helped by my instructor's laid back style which I can see now was less teaching and more of just going for a drive. The second time around I decided to go with one of the big names in driving schools, as I felt I needed the back up of an established brand to boost my faith in the lessons. I booked through their online system, choosing a time to suit me and the instructor gave me a call to introduce himself. All very straightforward.

If you don't want to, or don't have the funds to go with the big names, you can find independent instructors and smaller driving schools by searching online. And even though it didn't work for me, asking friends and family for recommendations is a good idea. Just make sure to find out as much as you can about what their lessons were like, and the instructor's teaching methods to see if they might be good for you too.

If you're paying someone to teach you to drive they must be either an approved driving instructor (ADI) or a trainee driving instructor. They will be regularly assessed and graded as either an A, B or fail. In 2017 the DVSA (Driver and Vehicle Standards Agency) launched an online search facility to help you find an approved driving instructor, where you can also see their grade if they choose to declare it. Enter your postcode and you'll get a list of instructors in your area. Bear in mind that driving instructors choose whether to be listed or not, so if yours doesn't appear, it doesn't necessarily mean anything bad. If you still want to check up on your instructor, you can do so by emailing or calling the DVSA directly.

Manual or Automatic?

When I thought about learning to drive, the concept of how to physically operate a vehicle was baffling to me. I could not comprehend being able to control a car and concentrate on the road at the same time. How could I possibly do all of that without careering into something or someone? Because of these concerns I considered taking my lessons in an automatic, but I eventually decided that I didn't want to limit myself and went with manual lessons. After a few weeks, changing gear became the least of my problems, and now it's a complete non-issue.

Personally, I'm glad I tried the manual lessons but if you feel an automatic is the best option for you then go for it. Just bear in mind you will only be able to drive an automatic when you pass, and they can be more expensive to buy and insure. Having said that, you may find you need fewer lessons as you won't be spending time on gears and clutch control.

Your Learning style.

The worst thing about my lessons the first time around, was that there was zero structure to them. My instructor would often arrive late, with no plan about what we were going to do that day and ask me to start driving. We'd amble along, while he chatted to me about his personal life, (his marriage was going stale and he hated his job) while I quietly worked myself in to a state of terror and anxiety. When I'm learning a new skill, I have to work through it step by step and know why I'm doing the things I'm doing. Have you ever been told that you will know when to change gear because "you'll just know"? Or that you'll get the hang of parking because "you'll just get a feel for it"? That way of learning was never going to work for me. When I met with my second instructor I explicitly told him "I don't know how to drive and I need you to teach me".

Perhaps your style of learning is more abstract or laid back, and that's fine, but be honest and frank with your instructor when you first meet them. Talk to them about what you need to make this work, and how you best learn. Your lessons should be planned, and then reviewed at the end of each session, with clear goals set about what you're going to work on next time.

The right person for the job

If you were having building work done to your house you would ask two or three people to give you a quote. You'd like to know about previous work they'd done and what makes them the best person for the job. The process of choosing your instructor shouldn't be much different. After all, you're about to invest a significant amount of money into this. Contact a few instructors and ask them some questions about their pricing, how they teach and what their pass rate is.

There seems to be an imbalance of power in the relationship between the student and driving instructor. The instructor holds the key to this new skill, and you are totally dependent on them teaching you. That's why you must constantly remind yourself that you are a paying customer and you have hired someone to do the job of teaching you to drive. Of course it takes a little time to establish whether this person is right for you, but if you've given it your best shot, and you find that it's just not working for you, don't be afraid to end that relationship and find someone new. I wish I had all those years ago. Instead, I ploughed on, awful lesson after awful lesson, my confidence slowly eroding away with each dreadful failure. If you find the right instructor for you, it will save you from a lot of stress, and a lot of expense.

Your instructor should:

- Turn up on time and give you the full one or two hours that you've paid for
- Take you back to your chosen destination at the end of each lesson
- Plan your lessons in advance and review what you've learned at the end of each one
- Have a calm and encouraging manner – they should make you feel at ease
- Listen to any feedback you have about how the lessons are going and consider any requests you have about what you'd like to learn

Your instructor should not:

- Ask you to stop at the shop/dry cleaners/bank or anywhere else for that matter during your lesson time
- Send texts or make phone calls during your lesson – you should have their undivided attention

- Pick up another pupil during your lesson in order to save themselves time (known as piggybacking)
- Make you feel uncomfortable in any way
- Expect you to automatically know what you're doing
- Shout at you when you make mistakes

Most people find an instructor that suits them and who provides a professional and reliable service.

But if you're really not happy with the service you're getting from you driving instructor, or their behaviour, you can complain to the DVSA. They will investigate your complaint and advise you on what to do.

"Price is what you pay. Value is what you get."

-Warren Buffet

Chapter 4. Keeping costs down

There's no getting away from the fact that learning to drive is expensive. In 2019 the cost of driving lessons varied between £20 and £30 per hour, and although the DVSA states that there is no minimum amount of lessons that you need to take to pass your test, most driving schools will tell you that you'll need around 45 hours. By the time you've factored in the price of the tests and any learning material you might want to buy the cost seriously mounts up.

However, there are some things you can do to soften the blow to your bank balance:

Swat up on the theory

Before you even begin your practical lessons, swat up on your theory to give you a head start. The more familiar you are with the rules of the road; the less time you'll need to learn this when you're actually in the car. You have to know this stuff for your theory test anyway, so you may as well get on with it.

Lessons with friends

I wouldn't personally recommend ditching the
professional lessons to save money, but having a few
lessons on the side if you can should definitely shorten the
time it takes you to master the skill and pass your test.
Choose this person wisely. Is your parent or partner really
the best person for the job? If you take criticism well and
they have the patience of a saint your relationship may
come out unscathed. Otherwise it will most definitely end
in tears. Also bear in mind that anyone willing to do this
must be over the age of 25 with a full valid driver's licence,
and you both must have the appropriate insurance in
place.

2 hours instead of 1

You'll probably be eager for the lesson to be over as
quickly as it possible, but think about booking a lesson that
lasts two hours instead of one. Although at first glance this
seems like a terrible idea (why prolong the agony?), you
may find that you're only just getting going by the time
your lesson ends. By extending it another hour, you're
maximising your learning potential, and anything that
does that improves your chances of passing sooner, saving

you money. Even if you don't do this every week, think about throwing in a two-hour session occasionally, particularly as you get closer to your test.

Block booking

This is a good idea as long as you've found the right instructor – that's paramount above all else. You don't want to be stuck with the wrong person because you've paid upfront for the next three months. Once you're confident you're in good hands, ask about any offers that cut cost if you book a number of lessons in advance.

Piggy backing

Your instructor should absolutely not be picking up the next student at the end of your lesson, and asking either you, or them, to drive you home with the other student as a passenger. This eats into your lesson time and when you've paid for a full hour or two, this cost adds up. Plus, you should have your instructor's undivided attention for the full session. Luckily this practice has become less common in recent years, but if you do find yourself with an instructor who suggests this, find a new one.

"When was the last time you did something for the first time?"

Chapter 5. The first lesson

Waiting for my instructor to arrive for my very first lesson I felt sick to my stomach. I hadn't slept the night before and didn't eat that morning. He arrived late and showed me to the passenger seat. He drove us around for an hour, chatting about various topics, some of which involved learning to drive, and when we arrived home he told my parents that from what he'd seen he expected me to pass very quickly. I hadn't even sat behind the wheel.

Several years later, at my second attempt to learn to drive, I sat waiting for my instructor to arrive for my first lesson. I felt surprisingly calm. I was of course apprehensive, but I had made up my mind that this time around I was going to be in control of the situation – I had paid for someone to take me out in a car and see if they could teach me to drive. The week before I had spoken to him on the phone and told him about my previous attempts, and that I just wanted to see how I felt about learning to drive again.

He arrived on time (much to my dismay. I was secretly hoping he wouldn't turn up and we could forget the whole thing). I got in the car and off we went. After introductions and a little small talk, I took the opportunity to tell him how I wanted these lessons to go and how I felt I would best learn. I needed clear, thorough instruction on everything, and even though I'd had some previous experience I wanted to start again from scratch.

We arrived at a quiet industrial estate and swapped seats. Oh Jesus. We went through the basics of seatbelts, seat and mirror position, and then he suggested that I might have a go at moving the car. Under his instruction, I slowly inched the car forward and came to a gentle stop. Again, slowly moving forward and then stop. "Ok let's move into second gear this time". And I did. Feeling quietly confident now I picked up the pace a little and then stopped, maybe a tad too abruptly, but all in all it had gone well, and I thought it a good idea to have a second lesson. As we sat and debriefed, a seagull flew overhead and launched an avalanche of crap all over the side of the car and the open passenger window, pebble dashing me and my instructor. Still feeling pleased with myself I saw it as a sign of good luck. ☺

So what should you expect from your first lesson?

You might not get the car into second gear on your first lesson, and hopefully you won't come away covered in bird crap, but you should expect the following:

Discuss your expectations and how you like to learn

You should have had some conversation about your learning style and expectations before even meeting your instructor, but if you haven't, now's the time to do it. Let them know how you like to learn. Maybe you're good with a laid back approach, where you're given an instruction and left to carry it out. Or perhaps you prefer detailed lesson plans and constant prompts about what you're supposed to be doing at any given time. Either way, your instructor should want to get to know you and how you learn before you're let loose on the roads.

Legal checks

Before you begin your lessons, your instructor will want to check that you're legally ok to drive as a learner driver. Have your provisional licence with you or you won't be going anywhere. They will also ask you to correctly read a licence plate parked 20m away, so if you normally need glasses or contacts, make sure you wear them for your lessons.

Cockpit Drill

Your instructor will drive you to a quiet, safe road and ask you to switch seats to the driver's side. You'll then run through the cockpit drill, which means checking your happy with how the car is set up before you set off. You'll need to do this each time you move off, and the way to remember each step is **DSSSM**:

D   **Doors.**

Check all doors are shut and secure

S   **Seat position for pedals.**

Slide the seat so that you can comfortably push the pedals all the way to the floor

S   **Seat adjustment**

Adjust the seat to comfortably reach the steering wheel and adjust the head rest to the correct position for you.

S   **Seatbelts**

An easy one. Make sure your seatbelt is on, and that your passengers have theirs on too. This includes your instructor!

M   **Mirrors**

Adjust your interior and door mirrors to get the best view.

Your instructor should explain each of these steps, including how to adjust the seats, and what the view in your mirror should look like to you. If you're not sure at any point, ask them to explain again, whether it's on your first lesson, or any future lessons. Remember that your instructor is there to teach you, even about something you might think should be obvious like how to adjust a car headrest.

Moving off

Once you've done all your checks and adjustments, it's time to move the car. As scary as that sounds, it's also pretty exhilarating the first time you do it. Also remember, your instructor will be in full control the whole time thanks to the dual controls, so you won't be able to do anything dangerous. They will talk you through how to use the handbrake, pedals and gears, and get you to slowly move the car forward. They'll also cover signalling, changing gears and how to come to a gentle and safe stop.

Towards the end of the lesson, your instructor will ask you to switch back to the passenger side, and will drive you home.

Debrief and plan next lesson

Perhaps you won't get as far as moving off the first time, or maybe you'll go a little further and move up a gear or two. Everyone is different, and you have to go at your own pace. As time goes on you'll want to make sure you're progressing, but for the first couple of lessons just let your confidence build and get used to the feeling of being behind the wheel of a car and in charge of a vehicle.

Whatever happens during the lesson, when you arrive home, your instructor should have left enough time for the two of you to discuss how you thought the lesson went, and what you'd like to achieve next time. This could be as much as repeating exactly what you just did, or moving things on a bit, but you should both agree this together.

After your first lesson, congratulate yourself and be happy with what you've just achieved. There's a way to go but if you take one lesson at a time you'll get there.

"You can't go back and change the beginning, but you can start where you are and change the ending."

– C.S. Lewis

Chapter 6. Making the most of your lessons

If I could go back and tell myself one thing about my driving lessons, it would be to make the most of the time I had each lesson. When I think about the time and money wasted, I could kick myself.

Each lesson would be more or less the same. My instructor would tell me to turn left here and take the second right there. I would do my best to follow instructions, and while I'm sure that just being a road user in general does have some merit in learning to drive, I now realise that I could have made much better use of that time by planning, asking questions and working on what I needed to the most. I would have enjoyed my time more. After all, learning a new skill is supposed to be enjoyable. It's scary to be out there in charge of a vehicle, but If you're taking professional lessons, you're being accompanied by a qualified professional who is in control of the car. You're in safe hands. I believe it's because we feel ourselves being judged by both our instructor and the people around us that our nerves take over. Have you ever been trying to parallel park, and you're getting along ok, only for a car to approach and completely throw you off?

Remind yourself that you're not doing this to be judged. You're doing this because it's a great life skill and a way of feeling empowered. Once again repeat your mantra that you are the customer in this situation. You've paid for a service and you want value for your money and time spent. Look at other areas of your life where you can make a comparison.

Imagine you have paid for a course of Spanish lessons. How are you going to spend those hours to get the most out of your time and ensure you reach your goal? You would most likely have a plan for each lesson, set goals and outcomes. If you mispronounced something, or couldn't quite remember last week's words, it's fine. Your teacher is there to guide you and prompt you. You certainly wouldn't be expected to know advanced conversations before you've learnt how to count, and you wouldn't spend the hour covering topics you already know and ignore the hard bits, hoping they'll never come up. If you didn't understand something you'd ask wouldn't you?

For the life of me I could not reverse around a corner. It seemed like the most difficult thing in the world to do.

Sometimes I'd get it, but that was more luck than skill, and I could have stayed quiet about it and just hoped it wouldn't come up on the test day. But I really wanted to learn to drive, not just pass a test, so I made it clear to my instructor that this magical corner reverse was eluding me, and we dedicated a couple of lessons to just that. By the end of a couple of weeks there was hardly a corner I hadn't reversed around. The problem is that if you ask family or friends about a specific problem such as this, particularly long experienced drivers, you are quite often told that you 'just judge it' or 'you just feel it'. This isn't all that helpful. Getting used to the feel and space of a car takes a long time - way after the time you pass your test. My instructor knew to give me specific advice and tools such as using my mirrors and reference points rather than blindly hoping for the best. And of course a lot of practice. The reverse around a corner manoeuvre has now been scrapped from the test, but I'm still glad I persisted in getting it cracked!

Speaking up during my lessons was definitely the most productive change I made. However, I made a conscious decision to not be quite so vocal about the very fact that I was taking lessons at all. Apart from my very close circle, I told on-one. I was able to take lessons on my day off, meaning no-one at work had to know. I didn't mention it to friends or post it on social media. Part of the reason I felt so bad about *not* being able to drive was the judgement and pressure from others. I wanted to keep this to myself and have total control over the situation, without the input of others, no matter how well meaning. This way I would be able to take my test without any expectations from others, and if I failed nobody had to even know.

I'd also come across an interesting concept called 'Social Reality Theory', a phenomenon which suggests you may be more likely to achieve your goal by keeping it to yourself. The idea is that when we share our plans and goals with our friends and family, we feel like we've already achieved something just by telling them what we're going to do. This is because it feels good to share and receive positive feedback from others, and this sense of satisfaction can somewhat replace the feeling of achievement you'd normally get from working towards your goal. Consequently, your motivation could dwindle, meaning you're less likely to commit to the work required. Everyone's different of course, and if you feel as though you need someone to encourage you and hold you to account when it comes to learning to drive, then share away, but perhaps keep sharing your news to a few trusted people rather than announcing it to the world.

Top tips for making the most of your lessons

What's the plan?

Together with your instructor you should have a lesson plan in place for each session, as well as an overall plan for achieving your outcomes over the coming weeks. You should end each lesson with a short debrief and review what you'll be looking at next time.

Book 2 hours instead of 1

We've already seen how this can save you money and let you really get your teeth in to something if you're finding it tricky. Try a longer session once in a while to give your learning a boost

Wear comfortable clothes and flat shoes

You want to feel relaxed and comfortable so ditch the heels and don't dress to impress

Be rested

Feeling fresh after an early night goes a long way, and absolutely no hangovers. Alcohol the night before can be dangerous so plan your nights out accordingly.

Speak up

If you don't understand something or a teaching technique isn't working for you, make sure your instructor knows about it. The sooner you mention it the sooner they can help.

Get a bird's eye view

If there's a tricky roundabout or junction with multiple lanes, I found it helpful to look at it from above using Google Earth. Being able to see how the road is mapped out gives you another perspective which can help make sense of where you need to be. I still use this now!

Calm those nerves

As with every stage of this process, you need to get a grip of your nerves, and that means losing that feeling of judgement of others, and reframing how you see your lessons. Put your faith in your instructor. It is their job to teach you and guide you, no matter how many times you get things wrong. Say your mantras, picture yourself as a confident driver and remind yourself that you are learning a new skill which takes time and effort.

"Success is stumbling from failure to failure with no loss of enthusiasm."

– Winston Churchill

Chapter 7. Making mistakes

Arriving home from each lesson, I tortured myself, going over and over in my head what had happened during the past hour. Cringing at how stupid I must look to my instructor, pointlessly chastising myself for not knowing how to drive already! This punishment wasn't only confined to when the lesson had finished. During the lesson, any mistake robbed me of all confidence, resulting in a tidal wave of mistake upon mistake. I'm now not ashamed to say that I cried in front of my instructor (on more than one occasion), but at the time I was mortified.

The truth is that we all make mistakes, and if you're not making any then you're probably not learning. For me, it again came back to viewing the lessons as a service that I'd paid for, and that the inevitable mistakes were all part of the learning process. As time went on I told myself that my instructor had seen this all before, and this was part of his job. Although I didn't entirely stopped worrying about making mistakes, changing how I viewed them definitely helped.

So here are a few of my howlers to make you realise you're not alone if you regularly mess up, along with some advice on how to deal with those awful moments where you want the ground to swallow you up.

During a mock test with my instructor, I came to a stop behind a queue of cars at a junction. I waited patiently for them to start moving on, but as the seconds turned in to minutes I began to wonder what was going on up ahead because we weren't moving anywhere. A van a few cars in front of me meant I couldn't quite see the front of the queue so I continued to wait. I glanced at my driving instructor who had a strange look on his face. This felt awkward. It turned out we weren't in a queue of traffic. We were sat behind a row of parked cars. Because we were doing a mock test, my instructor didn't say a word, and yes that would have been a fail.

Another event that sticks in my mind happened towards the end of an otherwise uneventful lesson as we approached a busy mini roundabout at the top of a hill, with the intention of turning right. There was a lot of traffic that night and as we inched along towards the front of the queue I began to feel increasingly nervous about what to do when we actually got there. Sure enough, this became a self-fulfilling prophecy. At the front of the queue, I waited for my opportunity to go, and when it finally came, I stalled. Overwhelmingly conscious of the massive line of cars behind me, all keen to get home after a hard day's slog, I desperately tried to remain calm as I started the car again and waited for another gap. I stalled again. And again. And again. Then the beeping started. After what felt like an eternity, I managed to get going again and made my way around the roundabout but by this time I'd worked myself into a complete panic. We pulled over and I was all for giving up for the day. Eventually I agreed to drive home which of course was the right thing to do but for a long time afterwards I avoided that roundabout.

The worst moments though have to be the ones where you think you actually could have caused an accident, or hurt someone. My worst happened towards the end of an otherwise non-eventful lesson. My instructor asked me to take the next left off a busy 40mph road. I was unfamiliar with the area, and wasn't clear on where that left was. I felt this pressure that I often get when I'm not sure what to do. A cyclist appeared alongside me and feeling panicked about missing the turn, I tried to turn left ahead of him. My instructor grabbed the wheel and guided me to stay where I was and told me to come off at the next left instead. It was a dangerous thing to do, and the realisation that I could have hit the cyclist, coupled with the shame of making such a big mistake when by now I should have known better meant that tears were inevitable. My face felt hot and I just couldn't hold it in. We stopped in a quiet cul-de-sac, and feeling absolutely mortified at the mistake, and embarrassed about crying, it was very difficult to get going again.

Looking back now, I'm actually glad that happened. If we sailed through all of our lessons, with no mistakes, how would we ever cope when something inevitably goes wrong when we've passed? I vowed to never repeat that mistake again, and came to the conclusion that it's a very GOOD thing to make mistakes with your instructor. That's literally what you're paying them for! You make mistakes and they teach you how to not make that mistake again. Also, they're able to step in with the dual controls and stop you from really cocking up. Far better to make a big mistake like this on a lesson, where you can be safe and learn from it.

As a learner driver you'll notice that other road users tend to beep if you take more than a millisecond to move off, or stall when the light turns green. They may even overtake you or drive too close to you. What you probably don't realise is that these same drivers will themselves stall on occasion, or miss a chance to pull out, because we're all human, and humans aren't perfect. It's just that they don't have a massive L slapped to the back of their vehicle.

Even when you've passed your test and are a fully-fledged driver, you will keep on making mistakes. Not huge, dangerous mistakes – if that's the case you wouldn't have passed your test. But you will stall, and you'll end up in the wrong lane or take the wrong exit. It's unlikely you'll be able to parallel park first time, and you'll probably seek out the easy parking spaces at first. (I still do). Hopefully, if you've had enough lessons and experience you'll be prepared to handle those mistakes and mishaps without too much drama. One such incident that springs to mind for me occurred not that long ago. During my usual commute to work, I gave way to a black car at a roundabout, and knowing how busy this roundabout gets, I took the opportunity to go straight after it. Feeling pretty pleased with how confident I'd been to see the gap and go for it, I glanced in the rear view mirror and noticed another very similar black car behind me. It slowly dawned on me that I'd unwittingly ended up as part of a funeral procession. With nowhere to stop for what seemed like forever, I crawled along in between the two grieving parties, wishing the ground would swallow me up, until at last I was able to pull over to the side and get out of their way. Mortified, I could have died.

So remember…

Making mistakes is good

That's how we learn. As the saying goes, you can't make an omelette without breaking a few eggs. And better to break those eggs while your instructor is there to help you clean them up ☺

They've seen it all before.

If you cry in front of your instructor, you won't be the first, and you won't be the last. If you need a break, ask to step outside the car for a few minutes while you get yourself together. But just know that there's nothing to be embarrassed about, and your driving instructor will understand.

You're the customer

Again and again it comes back to the fact that you've paid for these lessons, and mistakes are included in the cost. It's your instructor's job to help you learn from what you've done wrong so you can move on and do it right.

Move on

Reflecting on a mistake and learning from it is helpful, but torturing yourself by replaying the incident over and over in your head definitely isn't. If you really can't shake the 'what if' thoughts, try writing down what happened and what you'd do differently next time. I found that removing the thoughts from my head and on to paper helped me to move on.

Try to remember the Serenity Prayer, written by American theologian Reinhold Niebuhr:

God, grant me the serenity to accept the things I cannot change,
Courage to change the things I can,
And wisdom to know the difference.

"Feel the fear and do it anyway."

– Susan Jeffers

Chapter 8. The Test

This is what it's all been building up to. The Driving Test.

Looking back now, I am truly astonished that my first driving instructor put me forward for my practical test on any of the occasions that he did. I was in no way ready to drive unsupervised, and I cringe at what the examiner must have thought of the absolute disaster in front of him. I was quite rightly stopped from endangering myself and others when he turned to me each time and broke the dreaded news. My instructor should never have put me in that position, but because we were just winging it every lesson, there were no clear indicators of whether I was ready or not. Some lessons would go better than others, probably because nothing unexpected came up or the roads were quiet. It seems that because I'd completed a certain number of lessons, that was why I was taking the test. Whether I could be left alone in charge of a ton of metal hurtling along at 70mph was irrelevant. It's excruciatingly obvious now, but had the lessons been planned, and we'd been ticking off what I had or rather hadn't learnt, it would have saved a lot of time, money and disappointment. My confidence was battered and it

79

ingrained in me the idea that I would never be able to learn to drive for years to come.

Over the years the driving test has evolved and changed numerous times. Friends and family who took their tests in the 80's and 90's talk about a very different approach compared to today's standards. Up until 1996 there was no Theory Test. Instead, the examiner would ask the pupil questions about the Highway Code at the end of the test. Now of course the Theory Test is completely separate and at the time of writing consists of 50 multiple choice questions as well as the Hazard Perception Test. In fact, since I passed my own test there have been significant changes to the test such as the 'Show me, Tell me' vehicle safety questions, and the 'independent driving' section.

It's likely that the Theory and Practical tests will continue to change as new laws come in to force and driving conditions evolve. It goes without saying that you and your instructor should go through all aspects of the Theory and Practical tests in detail well before the day, and you should definitely be doing some mock tests in advance to make sure you're ready. There shouldn't be any surprises when it comes to what you need to achieve to pass. But one thing that hasn't changed over all the years, is test day nerves. On the day of my practical test the final time around, of course I felt nervous, but I also felt as ready as I could have been.

Control your nerves

In Chapter 3 we talked about how feeling nervous is normal but that you need to control and channel that stress to take advantage of its positive effects. Use this technique on the day of your test to give you the best possible chance.

Channel your nerves and use them for good. Tell yourself that the reason your heart is beating so fast is because of the adrenaline that your body is producing, to get you ready for the challenge ahead. This technique didn't completely stop me feeling nervous for my test, and I was literally shaking as I began, but I was able to slow down my breathing, carry on and get through it.

It's just an assessment

When it came to taking my test for the final time, I decided to stop calling it 'The Driving Test' and instead renamed it 'My Driving Assessment'. Much like changing the way I viewed stress, I changed the way I saw the test day. Rather than seeing the examiner as an all-powerful Judge, they would instead be my Assessor. I would be paying an expert to spend 40 minutes with me, to assess whether I was fully competent in the new skill I had been learning. I needed to know whether I was ready to drive a car on my own, and this was how I would find out. Reframing the test from being something which I had to pass, to being an assessment of how well I could drive gave me a sense of control which in turn softened the nerves.

Don't take your test before you are ready

You have to be ready to be a driver, not just pass the test. This is why the test has changed in recent years to include things like independent driving and questions about your knowledge of the car. Your instructor should have been teaching you how to be a driver, not how to pass a test. The test is just a way of proving you can do it.

There should come a point where you've done as much as you possibly can to prepare, and you've got a good chance of passing. Until then, don't rush to take the test.

The day of the test

You should arrange for your instructor to pick you up in plenty of time, and they will more than likely suggest an hour lesson beforehand to get you warmed up and go over any last minute niggles. For my first test, my instructor not only turned up late for my pre-test lesson, but then took me to get the car washed. Apparently he wanted it to look its best for my test!

Give yourself the best possible chance by getting some good rest the night before, and try to eat something to settle your stomach. Remind yourself that this is not a test of you as a person, but an assessment of your driving skills. If you pass this time, fantastic. If you don't, talk to your instructor about what you need to work on for next time, and don't leave it too long before getting back on the horse.

"The way I see it, if you want the rainbow, you gotta put up with the rain."

– Dolly Parton

Chapter 9. Life after lessons

When I started out on the journey of learning to drive, my absolute focus had been just to pass the test. That was the end goal, and to be honest I hadn't thought much beyond that. So when I did actually pass, I started to feel a sense of dread about what that actually meant and what I'd be expected to do next. I'd told almost no-one that I was learning to drive, and once I'd revealed the good news that I was a qualified driver, I'd probably be expected to get myself a car and *drive. On my own. Or worse still with passengers.* That thought was terrifying. As much as I used to hate telling people I couldn't drive, at least it was pretty cut and dry that I wouldn't be driving anyone anywhere. Now I could drive, I suppose I would be expected to actually do it? Having said that I must admit that I felt amazing telling friends and colleagues that not only had I been learning to drive but I had passed! First time! Well kind of, if you don't count the first three attempts ☺

I spent a bit too long avoiding buying a car of my own, because I knew that once I had one, that was it. I was a driver. Even though I had passed with only one minor fault, and even though my instructor told me I was a good driver, I still lacked the confidence to be on my own. And I'm so sorry to have to tell you this, but in my experience the only way to conquer the fear of driving is to drive.

I bought a car and set about becoming a proper driver. The problem was that I was still living within walking distance to my job and everywhere else I needed to be (a nice problem to have!), and so my poor car could sit unused and unloved for weeks on end! At one point the battery died because I hadn't been using it enough. The good thing (although it didn't feel like a good thing) about where I lived is that the parking was a nightmare, and so I became a dab hand at parallel parking. Although you could forget it if there was someone waiting behind me. No way was I going to park my car with someone watching. So there was a lot of driving around the block, looking for a suitable space with no-one looking. Now I live in an area where parking isn't quite so competitive, and my skills have dropped off somewhat.

After a while, my office relocated. It's a straightforward enough drive, with no motorways or complicated roundabouts, so it was a nice gentle start to get me used to doing a daily drive. I also had to navigate the school run, which is about as a cut throat as it gets when it comes to finding a parking space. I was pushing myself a little bit further every day.

My relationship with driving is still very much a work in progress. I look at other people who jump in their car and head off to wherever they're going without a second thought and think that will most likely never be me. I'll probably always be a reluctant driver, and the anxiety is always hanging around, but I can definitely say that it's getting better all the time and. I drive my commute and the school run without a second thought, and I travel a short distance down the motorway to visit my parents. There were busy routes and shopping centers I used to avoid because they overwhelmed me, but now I love the fact I can go there whenever I please, without needing someone to come with me or take two buses. I no longer panic about not being able to park. I know that I'll find somewhere, because experience has taught me that. I know what I need to do, and that's to keep pushing the boundaries of my comfort zone. Although I'm more than happy to drive a route I take every day, a new destination fills me with the same dread and stomach churning anxiety. I know that the only way to get over that fear is to face it.

Take it slowly

When I'm anxious, I panic and speed up. On an outing to a soft play centre with a very busy car park, I attempted to park in the first space I saw, believing that if I didn't get this space, there would be nowhere to park, we'd have to go home and the whole day would be ruined. The car park itself was narrow and there wasn't much room to manoeuvre. There was a queue of cars behind me and feeling under pressure I panicked, and swung the car into said space at a horrible angle, within an inch of hitting the car parked in the next to me. Panic took over and I couldn't for life of me figure out how to reverse back out without taking the neighbouring car with me. I felt like everyone was watching, waiting for the inevitable scraping of metal. Everything I did made it worse. I eventually managed to reverse back out, but by this time my heart was beating out my mouth and there were tears. If it wasn't for the small person in the back seat expecting a fun filled afternoon of soft play I'd have gone straight home.

So, my advice would be to **slow down**.

- Slow your speed down in places like car parks.
- Don't let other drivers put you under pressure. Keep going until you find a space you're comfortable with parking in.

- When you're performing a manoeuvre like parking, do it ever so slowly until you're more confident. If the angle isn't right, stop. Adjust what you're doing and try again.
- As your confidence grows, you'll feel ok with parking with an audience, and come to realise that people will just have to wait while you do your thing.

There will always be somewhere to park.

One of my biggest worries was that when I arrived at my destination, there would be nowhere to park. Then what would I do? Now I've been driving a fair while, I've realised that there is always somewhere to park. It may not be exactly where I wanted, and I may have had to drive around to find somewhere and then walk a little further to get where I needed to be. But I've yet to end up in a situation where I've driven somewhere and had to come home again because there's nowhere to park.

Other people can see you

Because you're the new guy at all this, it might feel like the only option open to you is to fit in with what everyone else is doing. If I wanted to change lanes for example, I felt like I had to wait for a gap, before I could move out. But what if I needed to change lanes, and there was no gap. I was forever destined to stay in my lane.

I confided to a friend that I dreaded motorway driving because of this problem. I stuck rigidly to the inside lane because changing lanes was so stressful. She agreed that yes, there would be times when changing lanes is easy because there's no-one at all in the other lane. There are also times when there are other vehicles in the lane that you want to move in to. And at those times you need to ask if you can move over, by indicating. Well that might sound pretty bloody obvious to everyone else, but this was a revelation to me. I suppose I did know this was a thing, of course I did, but I just needed someone to point it out in relation to my own driving experience. You're so insular when you first start driving, because you're desperately concentrating on your own actions, that you forget that you are part of a bigger picture. You'll start to notice that your fellow road users are not on a fixed collision course with you. So, check your mirrors, signal to indicate what you want to do, and when you're sure they're going to let you out, move in to the lane. Not so scary after all.

If you go wrong, stay wrong until you can make it right

There will be times where you find yourself in the wrong lane, or you've missed your exit. In my experience, the worst thing that you can do at this point is try to correct what you've done in a blind panic. Just continue on until you can calmly and safely find your way again. Come off at the next exit and turn back the other way, or carry on to the next roundabout and turn around. If you're really not sure what to do find somewhere safe to pull over so that you can reassess where you are and how to get back on course. Always try to have your phone fully charged and with you in case you need to call a friend or look up a map. If you have a smartphone you have access to a Sat Nav or route finder which is invaluable in these situations. You can prepare yourself as much as possible before you start your journey, by looking up your route and giving yourself plenty of time. You can even ask a friend to go with you on a trial run if it helps. But when you're going it alone for the first time remind yourself that if you go wrong, it's not the end of the world, because there will always be a way to make it right.

What do you do if you break down?

Because of my tendency to catastrophize, the thought of breaking down would cause me to have major anxiety. I've had my car for a few years now and have been lucky that it's stayed in pretty good shape, but I have experienced a flat tyre twice, and both times happened while I was driving. In fact, the first time I didn't even notice. Driving along with the window down, I could hear a weird clunking noise, and assuming there was something wrong but not knowing what, I decided to turn back from where I was going and drive home! Luckily I didn't cause any damage to the wheel itself. Even if you have 'run-flat' tyres (tyres designed to keep you moving as they resist deflation if punctured), it's recommended you only drive for a short distance at a lower speed, until you can get to a safe place to have your tyre changed. The second time it happened, I definitely knew about it, as my hub cap projectiled across the street when the tyre blew. I'd always thought I wouldn't know what to do in such a situation, but I slowed down, pulled over to the side of the road as soon as I could, and called for help. And then I walked back to retrieve my hub cap.

You can't predict when you might break down or get a flat tyre, but you can be prepared for it:

- Get breakdown cover. It will give you peace of mind. Keep the number on your phone and in the glove box.

- If you don't have breakdown cover, you can still ring and pay for instant cover, but it's probably going to cost more and take more time for them to reach you.

- Keep your car well maintained and have it regularly serviced.

- Make sure your phone is fully charged for emergencies.

- Have some warm clothes and a blanket in the car during the winter. You never know if you're going to be stuck for a long period of time in cold or wet weather.

- At the first sign of a problem, pull over to a safe place as soon as possible, and put your hazard lights on.

- If you're on a motorway or busy road, get out of your car on the left hand side, away from traffic and make sure all passengers do the same. Stand behind the crash barrier

- Don't try to change a tyre yourself unless you absolutely know what you're doing. A YouTube tutorial might make it look easy, but it can be dangerous, especially if you're on the side of a busy road or motorway. Many modern cars don't carry a spare tyre these days anyway.

What do you do if you have an accident?

You might not even want to think about this as a possibility, but it doesn't hurt to be prepared in case the unthinkable happens. Again, it was one of those things that caused me to have anxiety, because I hated the thought of being in a situation where I wouldn't know what to do. Nobody expects it to happen, but most people I know have been involved in a small bump or prang at one time in their life, and if you can know what to do if it happens to you, it will make the whole thing a bit easier to cope with. Just like a breakdown, you can't predict if an accident is going to happen, but regardless of who's to blame, these are a number of things you must do:

- Stop. You must stop, regardless of how minor the accident was; this is the law.
- Turn your engine off, put your hazards on and check if you or any passengers are injured.

- Call an ambulance and the police if anyone is hurt, or if the road is blocked.

- You should also call the police if the other driver leaves the scene, if you suspect alcohol or drugs have been taken, or if you think the accident was caused on purpose.

- Swap details – you need to share your name and address with everyone involved and they should do the same. You should also swap insurance details and the car registration details with the other driver. If they are not the owner of the car, you'll also need to get the details of whoever does. If for whatever reason you can't give your details at the time of the accident, you must report the accident to the police within 24 hours.

- As horrible as this sounds, don't apologise or admit fault. Even if it feels like it was your fault, it might not have been, and admitting fault verbally can be used against you if you later try to claim compensation.

- Before you leave the scene, try to note down as many details as you can, such as the colour and model of the other car, road conditions, the weather and any witnesses. If at all possible, take photos of any damage and of the scene around you. This could help with any insurance claim.

- However, minor the accident, you should report the accident to your insurance company. It doesn't mean you have to make a claim, but this will protect you later down the line if for example the damage turns out to be worse than you thought.

This might sound like a lot to take in, and if you are unfortunate enough to be involved in a car accident, you might feel a bit shaken and not able to focus on what you need to do. That's why I've included a checklist in the 'Useful Resources' section at the end of this book. You can download and print a free copy from the link provided. Keep it in your glovebox, along with a pen to take down details. Hopefully you won't need it, but if you do, at least you'll be prepared. ☺

Practice, practice, practice

Really and truly, the only way to get better at this is to keep doing it. It's something that I have to constantly tell myself. The truth is I've come further than I ever thought I would, but there's still so much more I could be doing. I'm super confident driving to work and the school run, and feel pretty good on short motorway runs that I'm used to. But I'm yet to jump in the car and head to a destination I don't know without some serious forward planning, and even then that familiar anxious feeling creeps back, and I have to remind myself of all of the above. The great thing about making one of these new trips is that I feel really good afterwards, and proud of myself for pushing that little bit further outside of my comfort zone. A fantastic book which I always recommend to people, is 'Feel the Fear and Do It Anyway' by Susan Jeffers. In it she explores how we can push our own boundaries a little further every day to gradually expand our comfort zones, until you're achieving things you might have previously thought impossible.

You've got this.

We may not all be natural born drivers, but I hope that by using some of the techniques and advice in this book, you're able to look at the process of learning to drive and driving itself with more confidence and a feeling of empowerment. Congratulate yourself on every small achievement and remind yourself before every lesson that you're in control of this journey. And when the day of your 'Driving Assessment' arrives, grab hold of those nerves and let the adrenaline focus your mind and propel you forward. This could be the day you become a fully-fledged driver, but if it's not to be, there's always next time, and you'll be ready. So good luck to you ☺

Useful Resources

Follow mw on twitter for regular updates and free tools and resources **https://twitter.com/JumpStartDriver**

Download the free accident checklist (also printed at the end of this book) **https://bit.ly/30XtJOV**

www.anxietycare.org.uk Anxiety Care UK is a community organisation dedicated to supporting people with anxiety disorders.

https://www.gov.uk/learn-to-drive-a-car Step by step guide of the practicalities of learning to drive, including online search facility to find an instructor and online booking facility for theory and practical tests.

Jeffers, S. (2007) **Feel the Fear and Do It Anyway**. Revised Edition. Vermillion

www.mind.org.uk Mind provides advice, and support to anyone experiencing mental health problems. A wealth of information about mental health including anxiety disorders.

www.nhs.uk/conditions/phobias NHS definition and overview of the meaning of phobias, plus information regarding the symptoms, causes and treatments available.

www.time-to-change.org.uk Time to Change is a growing social movement working to change the way we all think and act about mental health problems. Read and share personal stories and blogs.

ACCIDENT CHECKLIST ☑

My details (complete in advance)
Insurance company: ....
Policy number: ....

Immediate Action
☐ Turn hazard lights on
☐ Check everyone for injuries
☐ Call the police and ambulance if people are hurt
☐ Call the police if:
☐ The road is blocked
☐ The other driver leaves the scene
☐ You suspect alcohol or drugs have been taken
☐ You suspect the accident was purposely caused

Other driver details
☐ Name: ....
☐ Address: ....
☐ Phone number: ....
☐ Insurance details: ....
☐ Car Reg: ....
☐ Witness details: ....

Accident details
☐ Date: .... Time: ....
☐ Location: ....
☐ Car Model: .... Colour: ....
☐ Road conditions: ....
☐ What happened? ....
  ....
☐ Take photos if possible

Report to:
☐ Your insurance company
☐ The police within 24 hours

Printed in Great Britain
by Amazon

36389300R00064